DOG CALLED BOB

Balboa Press books may be ordered through booksellers or by contacting:

Balboa Press
A Division of Hay House
1663 Liberty Drive
Bloomington, IN 47403
www.balboapress.com
1 (877) 407-4847

Because of the dynamic nature of the Internet, any web addresses or links contained in this book may have changed since publication and may no longer be valid. The views expressed in this work are solely those of the author and do not necessarily reflect the views of the publisher, and the publisher hereby disclaims any responsibility for them.

Any people depicted in stock imagery provided by Getty Images are models, and such images are being used for illustrative purposes only.
Certain stock imagery © Getty Images.

ISBN: 978-1-9822-3208-5 (sc)
ISBN: 978-1-9822-3209-2 (e)

Library of Congress Control Number: 2019910613

Print information available on the last page.

Balboa Press rev. date: 04/20/2020

BALBOA
PRESS
A DIVISION OF HAY HOUSE

Renae Jeffrey

This is my dog,
His name is Bob.

Bob can jump,
He lands with
a thump.

Bob can do
tricks,
He can fetch
sticks.

Bob tried to impress,
He just made
a big mess.

Bob is the
one I love,
He ate my new
baseball glove.

Bob dug up
the fennel,
He was sent
to his kennel.

Bob started
to moan,
He ate his bone.

Bob is great,
He is my
best mate.

Stick Photos of You and Your Special Friend

Stick Photos of You and Your Special Friend

Draw Pictures of You and Your Special Friend

Draw Pictures of You and
Your Special Friend